BE AN EFFECTIVE COMMUNICATOR

SPEAKING WITH CONFIDENCE

AMY B. ROGERS

New York

Published in 2022 by The Rosen Publishing Group, Inc.
29 East 21st Street, New York, NY 10010

Copyright © 2022 by The Rosen Publishing Group, Inc.

Portions of this work were originally authored by Jennifer Landau and published as *The Right Words: Knowing What to Say and How to Say It*. All new material in this edition authored by Amy B. Rogers.

First Edition

All rights reserved. No part of this book may be reproduced in any form without permission in writing from the publisher, except by a reviewer.

Library of Congress Cataloging-in-Publication Data

Names: Rogers, Amy B., author.
Title: Speaking with confidence / Amy B. Rogers.
Description: New York : Rosen Publishing, [2022] | Series: Be an effective leader | Includes index.
Identifiers: LCCN 2021031849 (print) | LCCN 2021031850 (ebook) | ISBN 9781499470321 (library binding) | ISBN 9781499470314 (paperback) | ISBN 9781499470338 (ebook)
Subjects: LCSH: Social skills--Juvenile literature. | Interpersonal relations--Juvenile literature. | Communication--Juvenile literature.
Classification: LCC HQ783 .R647 2022 (print) | LCC HQ783 (ebook) | DDC 302.2--dc23
LC record available at https://lccn.loc.gov/2021031849
LC ebook record available at https://lccn.loc.gov/2021031850

Manufactured in the United States of America

Some of the images in this book illustrate individuals who are models. The depictions do not imply actual situations or events.

CPSIA Compliance Information: Batch #CWRYA22. For further information, contact Rosen Publishing, New York, New York, at 1-800-237-9932.

CONTENTS

INTRODUCTION — 4

CHAPTER 1
CONNECTING WITH CLASSMATES — 7

CHAPTER 2
SPEAKING WITH ADULTS AT SCHOOL — 21

CHAPTER 3
FAMILY TIES — 35

CHAPTER 4
FRIENDSHIP AND DATING — 47

CHAPTER 5
THE WORDS TO USE AT WORK — 59

GLOSSARY — 70

FOR MORE INFORMATION — 72

FOR FURTHER READING — 74

INDEX — 76

INTRODUCTION

Words matter. They're the backbone of communication—the sharing of thoughts, ideas, and feelings. The words we say to others can build and break relationships, open doors along our career path, and even help change the world. From big speeches in front of crowds to conversations among friends and serious discussions with teachers or parents, the words we say carry weight. They matter.

This is why it's important to think before you speak. It's easy to just say the first thing that comes to mind, but the first thing often isn't the right thing. When we don't choose our words carefully, it can cause misunderstandings and even hurt feelings. However, when we take a moment to collect our thoughts and speak from a calm, confident place, we can do our best to make sure we're communicating clearly with others.

Speaking with confidence isn't always easy. When we have to give a presentation at school, ask a teacher for help, set boundaries with our family, or ask someone on a date, it can be hard to find the right words. The anxiety it causes might be so bad it makes us not want to talk at all! However, practice makes perfect—especially when it comes to speaking. The more we practice speaking in different situations, the more comfortable we become.

Speaking is a skill—just like writing and listening. That means we can learn helpful tips to get better at it over time. Learning about the different ways to communicate with different groups can help us tailor our message and the way we deliver it to our audience. For example, the way you speak to your friends or siblings about a problem is likely very different from how you address a teacher, parent, or boss. Knowing how to speak clearly and confidently in a variety of situations is one of the keys to being an effective communicator.

Some people might think speaking confidently means talking down to others. However, that's not the case at all. Instead, someone who speaks with confidence doesn't need to speak in a patronizing, mean, or aggressive way to make themselves feel good. They know when and how to apologize, ask for help, and support others. Confident speakers often inspire others and are good at comforting and helping people through their words. They know that it's better to build people up through the things they say than to tear them down.

Speaking with confidence can lead to success in many areas of life. It might seem as if strong speaking skills are only helpful if you want a career as a politician,

SPEAKING WITH CONFIDENCE

When people think of confident speakers, they often think of leaders like Barack Obama, whose speeches inspired people before, during, and after his time as president. However, anyone can be a confident speaker if they spend enough time learning and practicing.

actor, or CEO. However, these skills aren't just put into action when we're speaking in front of big groups of people. Public speaking skills are very useful, but it's just as important to be an effective speaker in one-on-one situations. That's how we make friends, strengthen family ties, and establish good relationships with our bosses and coworkers. From the classroom to a first date, every situation becomes easier when we feel more confident speaking with others.

Words matter, and when we learn to speak with confidence, we learn to find the right words for each situation and to say them the right way so our audience knows exactly what we mean. That's what being an effective communicator is all about!

CONNECTING WITH CLASSMATES

CHAPTER 1

You spend a lot of your time at school. That makes it a great place to practice your speaking skills. In the classroom, the cafeteria, and the halls, you're likely to meet and interact with many different kinds of people. Some of them will become your closest friends, some will be people you work with on group projects or as lab partners, and some might even be people you don't get along with at all. It's important to know how to communicate with all of these different types of classmates. You have to spend a lot of time with them, so it's good to learn how to work together to meet goals, make friends, and deal with bullying behavior.

SPEAKING WITH CONFIDENCE

Not everyone you meet at school is going to become your best friend, but it's still important to speak to them with respect and empathy, while respecting yourself too.

It's important to approach most interactions—especially with your peers—from a place of empathy. This means trying to understand another person before judging them. Even if you don't know a classmate well or if your group project partner seems like they have a perfect life, it's never helpful to make assumptions about someone you need to communicate with. Instead, speaking to them in an open, friendly, and clear way—and listening actively when they speak to you—can help you both get to know each other better and find common ground.

Confident speakers often use their words to connect with others, and they generally work to make sure these connections are positive ones. They're not bullies. In fact, confident speakers know how to use their communication skills to deal with bullying behavior and make spaces like school safer and better for everyone around them.

PUBLIC SPEAKING AT SCHOOL

When you think of speaking with confidence in the classroom, one of the first things that might come to mind is giving a speech or presentation. You might be asked to deliver a book report in front of your class, to give a presentation about a person in history, or to deliver a speech before student council elections. Some schools even have public speaking classes that students can take as an elective or must take as part of the curriculum.

For some people, even just the idea of speaking in front of their class or their whole school makes them feel anxious, and that's perfectly normal. It can be scary to speak in front of a crowd. However, if you have to give a presentation or speech, it's helpful to be prepared and to practice. Being as prepared as possible by learning as much as you can about what you're going to be talking about, writing out notes or even your whole speech, and taking care of your body (by eating, drinking water, and getting enough sleep before your speech) can help you feel more confident. In addition, delivering your speech in front of a mirror, practicing in front of friends or family, or videotaping yourself can help you take note of any stumbling blocks, work on your use of gestures, and make sure you're not speaking too loud, soft, fast, or slow.

When you get up to deliver your speech, it's helpful to make eye contact with people in the audience, stand up tall, and remember to breathe. Reminding yourself that you know what you're talking about and that your classmates want to see you succeed can give you the confidence boost you need to get a good grade on your presentation or win the class election on the strength of your speech. Public speaking may seem scary, but it can also be rewarding!

WORKING TOGETHER

Another time it's important to speak with confidence at school is when you're working on a group project or an assignment with a partner. This can be a stressful situation, especially if you're paired with a group or an individual you're not friends with or don't know very well. However, it's

CONNECTING WITH CLASSMATES

Public speaking is an important life skill, and it's good to practice it at school.

11

The Basics of Body Language

The words we use when we speak are only one of the ways we communicate our thoughts and feelings to those around us. Another important form of communication is nonverbal communication, which is also known as body language. Nonverbal communication involves the facial expressions we make, the gestures we use, the way we stand, and even our tone of voice. In some cases, these enhance the message we're sending with our words. In other cases, they reveal our true feelings when our words are saying something else.

For example, if you're running for class president, you might give a speech in which you say you're happy to be addressing your classmates. However, if you're looking down with your shoulders hunched while nervously drumming your fingers on the podium, you won't look happy. You'll look nervous and unsure. Body language is such a big part of communication that people often take the messages it sends as the truth over someone's words whenever those two things contradict each other.

Paying attention to your body language is a big part of speaking with confidence. If you notice that you play with your hair when you're nervous, you can take that awareness and change that habit to appear more confident. You can hold your hands at your sides instead of playing with your hair. This makes you look less anxious.

Speaking in front of a mirror or asking a trustworthy friend to point out any nervous gestures can help you realize the little things you do without even thinking about them that might cause you to appear less confident in conversation. Then, you can work to change those habits and replace them with ones that make you look and feel more sure of yourself.

helpful to remember that you're all working together toward the same goal—to complete the assignment and to get a good grade.

One of the most important parts of a group or partner project is clearly communicating the roles each person needs to fulfill. If you feel your strengths would make you a good fit for a certain part of the project, share that with the person or people you're working with. For example, if part of the project involves making a video and you enjoy making short movies on your computer, you can let your group members know that you'd like to take charge of that part of the assignment.

As the roles are being assigned, make sure they're being assigned evenly so no one ends up with too much work. If you feel you've been given an unfair workload or a task you're not comfortable with, speak up right away. This can keep you from falling behind or resenting your group members later. In addition, once you're given your task, verify it with your other group members to make sure you know exactly what your job is and when you need to have it done, and if one of your group members asks you about their responsibilities, clearly outline their role and any dates they need to remember for deadlines.

Sometimes, even if the workload is divided fairly at the beginning, someone falls behind on their part or doesn't contribute as you thought they would. When approaching a classmate who has fallen behind on their part of a project, don't belittle them. They may be confused or overwhelmed and too embarrassed to approach you or ask for help. Instead, approach them from a place of empathy and ask if they need help or have any questions about their part of the assignment. If they are simply looking for someone else to take over their work, though, it's important to firmly remind

Group projects can be hard, but clear communication can make the process smoother for everyone involved. In addition, writing down everyone's responsibilities and making sure everyone has a copy of this information can help clear up any confusion.

CONNECTING WITH CLASSMATES

them what they need to do and what date they need to have it done by. Stick to the facts and the plan you established when the assignment was given, and don't raise your voice or let your anger keep you from clearly communicating what needs to be done. If you have to bring the teacher into the discussion, which can sometimes happen, stay calm and focused on the project at hand and not your clashing personalities.

HOW TO STOP TEASING AND BULLYING

School can be a place to make great friends. However, it can also be a place where you have to deal with less friendly forms of communication. Teasing and bullying are problems many students face at school, and it can be hard to know how to handle these issues. In some cases, it might feel easier to just ignore it and hope the teasing stops or the bully gets bored. Sometimes this approach

SPEAKING WITH CONFIDENCE

Physical bullying involves any act of physical harm against someone else. Social bullying includes spreading rumors, publicly embarrassing someone, or purposely excluding somcone from social situations. Verbal bullying includes saying mean things and threatening physical harm. Cyberbullying is bullying done through the internet, text messages, and other digital forms of communication.

works. However, if someone says something that makes you feel uncomfortable or hurt—even if it's just a joke—you don't have to ignore it or laugh it off. Speaking with confidence includes speaking up for yourself. Being treated with kindness is something everyone deserves, and if you're being treated unkindly, it's important to make it known that you don't like it.

One of the most effective ways to clearly communicate that you don't like what someone is saying when they're teasing you is to use an I-message, which is also known as an I-statement. This is a way of speaking that focuses on the beliefs or feelings of the speaker. For example, if a classmate has been teasing you for a few days in a row about tripping in gym class and you want them to stop, you can say, "I don't think it's funny, and I feel hurt when you keep bringing it up. Please stop." This makes your feelings clear and directly states what behavior is causing you to feel hurt.

Teasing can make you feel sad, angry, or anxious. However, it's not the same as bullying. Bullying involves a repeated pattern of aggressive behavior that can inflict both emotional and physical harm. Teasing is also often done between friends, who are equals. Bullying is related to an imbalance of power. This can mean a bully is stronger than their victim physically, is more popular socially, or has access to pictures, embarrassing stories, or other private information that gives them power over their victim. Most schools have policies against bullying, but it still happens to many students on a daily basis.

If you're being bullied, it can be hard to know how to respond. Confidence is important, but you don't want to be seen as so aggressive you're looking to start a fight. If a bully says something mean or threatening to you, be clear and direct, and focus on their behavior rather than picking on them in retaliation. Make statements such as "It's not OK to talk to me that way" or "What you're saying isn't true, and you need to stop." A firm, even tone of voice and steady eye contact will project confidence. You may not feel confident, but acting as if you do will help you communicate from a position of strength. If the bully continues lashing out, walk away. You never want to get involved in what could become a fight.

Any kind of threat made by a bully should be taken seriously, and you shouldn't have to handle it on your own. Talk to a trusted adult as soon as possible, and give them all the information you have about what's been said or done to you. Although you may feel embarrassed, remember that you have done nothing wrong. If a bully threatens to harm you if you tell anyone, let that be known as well. A big part of communicating effectively is being able to advocate for yourself and clearly state your needs in a given situation. In this case, your safety is an important need, so asking for help is the best thing you can do.

MAKING YOUR SCHOOL SAFER

Even if you're not being bullied yourself, you can use your words to help stop bullying behavior. Peer intervention, which happens when classmates step in to stop a bully or tell them what they're doing is wrong, is one of the most effective ways to combat bullying in school. Most bullies expect bystanders to look the other way, but if you and your classmates band together, you can help change the culture of your school.

A great place to start is by giving verbal support to the person being bullied. Bullies often work hard to make their victims feel alone, but just by talking to someone who's being bullied, you can make them feel like someone has their back. Make it clear that you don't agree with the bully's words or actions and that you want to help.

If you feel comfortable talking with a bully directly, keep your voice calm and even. Don't go into a long discussion or try to be confrontational. A comment such as "Please stop being so mean to David. It's not cool, and I'm sure you wouldn't want to be treated that way" is enough. If you can, encourage your fellow classmates to do the same. The idea is not to gang up on the bully but to let them know that others disapprove of the bullying. If there is no reasonable way to approach the person, enlist the help of a teacher, a counselor, or another trusted adult at school.

DEALING WITH YOUR FEELINGS

Whether you're dealing with a bully who's picking on your friend, telling a classmate to stop teasing you about a boy who likes you, or having trouble getting someone to pull their weight in a group project, one of the biggest keys to communicating with confidence at school is learning to control strong emotions. We all have big feelings sometimes—such as anger, anxiety, frustration, or embarrassment—and it's healthy to have them and acknowledge them. However, negative emotions can sometimes get in the way of effective communication. You can't communicate well if your heart is pounding because you're angry, if your stomach is in knots because you're anxious, or if you start to cry because you're frustrated.

It can be hard to feel these feelings without letting them control you or affect how you speak to others. However, it's important to take steps to deal with negative emotions before you speak to someone else. First, acknowledge what you're feeling. Being able to tell yourself "I feel very angry right now" is important because it gives you some power over what you're feeling. Then, take a few deep breaths to calm both your body and your mind. Finally, saying a calming statement to yourself, such as "I can deal with this," is helpful. It allows you to focus on what you can control. You may not be able to control how something makes you feel, but you can control what you do with those feelings. By taking a moment to deal with your emotions before you speak, you'll be better able to communicate clearly, calmly, and confidently in any situation.

SPEAKING WITH ADULTS AT SCHOOL

Your classmates aren't the only people you interact with at school. There are a variety of adults you speak to throughout the day—from your teachers and guidance counselors to your volleyball coach or the director of your school play. Learning how to effectively communicate with these adults—including both what to say to them and how to say it—can help make your experiences at school positive and successful.

It takes time, practice, and active listening to learn how to best communicate with all the different people you come across. It's helpful to know what your goal is in a discussion so you can decide how to approach the conversation to meet that goal. For example, your goal might be to convince your teacher to give you an assignment to earn extra credit, or it might be to learn a better free-throw shooting technique from your basketball coach.

Speaking with adults is not the same as speaking with your peers or people younger than you. Coming into each conversation from a place of respect is important, but it's also important to know that respecting authority figures doesn't mean you should let them treat you poorly or abuse their power. If you feel this is happening, clearly communicate these concerns to another trusted adult.

TALKING TO YOUR TEACHERS

Teachers are often the adults you speak to the most at school, and learning how to discuss different things with them is an important

SPEAKING WITH ADULTS AT SCHOOL

People who speak with confidence know that how they speak can—and often should—change depending on their audience. For example, they wouldn't joke around with their basketball coach as freely as they would with their teammates. They'd treat their coach with more respect and less familiarity.

SPEAKING WITH CONFIDENCE

It might seem scary or embarrassing to ask a teacher for help, but that's their job! If you clearly communicate what you're struggling with or any questions you have, they can give you the advice, tips, and tools you need to succeed.

SPEAKING WITH ADULTS AT SCHOOL

part of being successful in the classroom. When a teacher asks a question you know the answer to, it's polite to raise your hand and wait to be called on instead of shouting out the answer. This is also what you should do if you have a question you'd like your teacher to answer during class. Interrupting them or another classmate isn't respectful behavior. In addition, if a teacher calls on you to answer a question you don't know the answer to, try not to get defensive. It's often best to admit you don't know the answer so your teacher can help you understand the material better.

If you have a more serious concern you need to address with your teacher, schedule a meeting at a time that works for both of you. Students are more likely to get their teachers' full attention this way, and most teachers respond

Conversations with Coaches

Coaches generally want to help their players succeed and should be given the same respect as teachers. In fact, many coaches for school sports teams have a full teaching schedule along with their coaching duties. In addition, coaches for travel teams and town teams, dance teachers, musical directors, and any other people who teach or coach you outside of school should also be spoken to with respect.

Sometimes concerns come up about a coach playing favorites or being unfairly critical. These concerns should be addressed using I-messages. Saying "You act like Courtney is the only player on the team who matters" will only make the coach feel attacked. A comment such as "I feel frustrated that I'm not getting more playing time and wish you would give me a chance to prove myself" will make the coach more likely to hear you out.

If you don't make the team in the first place, ask to meet with the coach to discuss how you can improve your chances for the following season. Whining, scowling, or standing with your arms crossed in front of your chest will not make a good impression. Instead, adopt an open stance, use a calm tone of voice, and ask thoughtful questions about how to prepare to try again.

There may come a point when you need to quit a sports team for whatever reason. It's far better to be honest with your coach about this decision, rather than to just stop showing up for practice. It's fair to give a brief explanation, but there's no need to go into great detail. Keep it short, and focus on the positives. However, if you're quitting because of problems on the team that you feel need to be addressed, scheduling a meeting in which you bring up your concerns in a direct but respectful manner is a good plan of action.

favorably to this kind of initiative. When you speak to your teacher, be clear about any problems you're having in class. Never belittle your teacher when discussing why you're having issues with a particular subject. Saying "You didn't explain that math problem well" isn't as effective as saying "I didn't understand how you solved the math problem you used as an example today." I-messages work well in this kind of setting because it puts the focus on the speaker rather than putting the blame on the listener.

When your teacher explains a concept to you, write it down, and then repeat it back to make sure you understood what was said. In addition, if you have any more questions or still don't fully understand the topic, don't get frustrated. Take a moment to breathe and collect your thoughts, and then ask about the specific issues you're still having or the specific questions you still need answered.

There is no shame in asking for help from a teacher after class or for asking for more clarification in the classroom. When teachers ask if anyone has questions after they explain a concept, it's because they want to make sure everyone understands the material, so if you still have a question, don't be afraid to ask it. Chances are, you're not the only one in your class who needed it answered.

COMMUNICATING WITH GUIDANCE COUNSELORS

A guidance counselor is another important person you should know how to communicate with at school. They often have more specific training than teachers do in terms of

SPEAKING WITH CONFIDENCE

In addition to guidance counselors, some schools employ psychologists to help students who are dealing with mental health concerns. These people are helpful resources, and you should never feel afraid or ashamed to talk to them about problems you have or anxiety you feel.

SPEAKING WITH ADULTS AT SCHOOL

dealing with the issues young people face—from school stress and bullying to trouble at home. Meeting with a guidance counselor is one instance where you don't have to know exactly how to say what's on your mind. You only need to know how to begin, which is by sharing what's bothering or worrying you. A guidance counselor will often work with you as you sort through your thoughts and feelings.

It's important to be honest when talking with a guidance counselor. If you are worried about a college application or sad because your father lost his job, say so. Trust that the guidance counselor will be sympathetic to your concerns. They know

SPEAKING WITH CONFIDENCE

10 Great Questions TO ASK A GUIDANCE COUNSELOR

1. I've been feeling very anxious about the future lately, and it's been affecting my schoolwork. What can I do to feel better and regain my focus?

2. I've noticed people picking on the new transfer student a lot lately. How can I get them to stop?

3. I'm being bullied by one of the people in my gym class. Can you help me?

4. Do you have any tips for acing a college scholarship interview?

5. How can I tell my teacher that I don't think it's fair that she punishes the whole class when only one person does something wrong?

6. My football coach has been punishing one person for every bad play—even when it's not their fault. What can I say to get my coach to stop?

7. How do I tell my parents I want to go away for college when they've always said they want me to stay at home?

8. My parents are getting divorced and are saying mean things about each other. Is there a way to talk to them about this without choosing sides?

9. My best friend's mom passed away recently. What can I say to help her get through this hard time?

10. My friend said she's thought about hurting herself. Whom can I talk to in order to make sure she gets the help she needs?

that most students who come to see them are coming with problems, so don't worry about needing to ease into the conversation. Clearly share your concerns or questions, and then try your best to honestly answer any questions they may ask you about how you feel or what you want to do next.

It's normal to be worried that news of your problems will get back to your classmates or teachers. This is especially true if you're talking to a guidance counselor about problems with a teacher or an issue in your friend group. Tell your guidance counselor about these concerns, but know that most schools have confidentiality agreements in place. However, if your counselor becomes aware of a potentially dangerous situation, they will have to take action to ensure that no one is hurt and everyone stays safe. In most cases, though, what you share is kept private. Keeping this in mind can allow you to communicate without fear and to openly share what's bothering you. That trust is an essential part of the relationship between students and counselors, and it's something that's often needed for effective communication in other areas of life, too, especially about sensitive subjects.

ASKING FOR HELP

Your guidance counselors at school are there to help, but sometimes you might feel more comfortable sharing your concerns with another adult, such as a teacher, a coach, or a club moderator. It's important to have someone you can go to when you need to ask for help. However, it's also

SPEAKING WITH CONFIDENCE

At first, it might feel uncomfortable to talk about your problems at school, but it's healthier to ask for help than to struggle alone. If you're having a hard time but don't feel comfortable talking to a guidance counselor or school psychologist, you can go to your favorite teacher or coach first.

important to remember that some problems, especially ones that involve your safety, the safety of another student, or mental health concerns, might be too serious for someone without professional training or expertise to handle on their own. If you tell your favorite teacher that a bully has said they're going to hurt you and your teacher goes to a higher authority such as the principal, they're not trying to betray your trust. They're simply trying to get you the help you need.

Asking for help from an adult at school—whether it's asking your teacher to explain a chemistry concept more clearly or asking your coach if they can work with you on catching fly balls in the outfield—can be scary. It's hard to admit when we need help, and we often want the adults we interact with to be impressed by us and think we're mature. However, the most mature thing anyone can do is clearly and confidently communicate their needs, including their need for someone to help them when they're having a hard time.

This is especially true in terms of your mental health. If you're feeling depressed or anxious, asking for help from a mentor, guidance counselor, or psychologist can feel like you're admitting that you're weak. However, it's actually a sign of strength. It takes courage to say "I'm not doing OK right now, and I think I need help," but it's the best thing you can do when you feel bad. Everyone needs help sometimes, and learning to ask for it in different areas of our lives—from school to our families—is one of the most important ways we can use our communication skills.

FAMILY TIES

Long before you started going to school, the first group of people you learned to communicate with was your family. That doesn't always mean they're the easiest group to talk to, though. Some people feel they can tell their parents, guardians, siblings, and other family members anything. Others don't always feel comfortable sharing things with their family members.

Sometimes communication struggles in families develop because everyone is busy. Between work, school, practices, and homework, it can be hard to find time to spend together to talk about your day and ask how each other is doing. It's helpful to work together to plan times to enjoy each other's company, such as a weekly game night or Sunday dinner. It's also important to take small moments to communicate to your family members that you care about them. This could be something as simple as asking your mother how her big meeting went or telling your sister you're proud of her for making the dance team at school. Using your words to show others you're paying attention to what's happening in their lives and that

Family dinners are a great way to talk as a family about your lives. However, it can be hard to make time for these kinds of moments, and it's OK if your family struggles sometimes to stay involved in each other's lives. It might take a little more effort for you to check in with one another when you're all so busy, but you can still stay connected.

they matter to you is an essential part of effective communication among family members.

In some cases, communication problems in families happen because of deeper issues, such as divorce, abuse, or an inability for family members to accept part of a person's identity. For example, a young person who's a member of the LGBTQ+ community might not feel comfortable talking to their parents about someone they're dating because their parents aren't supportive of them. Sometimes it's helpful for families to go to counseling or therapy to develop stronger communication skills in these instances. However, if your family is not open to this path, it's OK to talk to friends, other relatives, or another trusted adult such as a teacher about things you don't feel comfortable sharing with your parents, guardians, or siblings. Every family struggles with communication at times, and finding the best and safest way to communicate your needs, concerns, and problems is an important part of speaking with confidence.

HAVING HARD CONVERSATIONS

Even if you have a great relationship with your parents or guardians, there are still some topics that aren't always easy to bring up—from a bad grade in chemistry class to something even bigger like your gender identity. When you need to approach a parent, stepparent, or guardian about an issue, plan ahead. Think about your goal for the conversation. Having a sense of what you need ahead of time will help focus the discussion.

Knowing when to approach someone is vital too. It's not a good idea to ask a family member to have a heart-to-heart about a conflict with a friend while they're rushing out the door to work. Instead, it's best to approach them when they have time to focus. Say, "I need to talk to you about something. Do you have time to talk now?" Showing that level of respect will start the conversation off on the right foot.

When you speak about what's on your mind, don't rush. You may have been obsessing about the dance you want to take a girl to for weeks, but this is the first your parents are hearing about it. They need time to process the information and come up with a response. Speak in a calm, even tone of voice,

Some families have found that holding family meetings helps them solve problems or address issues before they spin out of control.

and try to maintain eye contact while speaking. In addition, approach the conversation from a place of empathy and openness rather than defensiveness. In many cases, this will make the adults you're talking to respond to you with that same empathy and openness. There may be a concert your friend wants you to go to with him that would cause you to miss your curfew. Calmly asking to stay out an extra hour is more likely to get a favorable response than demanding to come home three hours late.

If you don't get the response you were hoping for, try not to react from a place of anger. Take a deep breath, collect your thoughts, and try to understand the other side. You can suggest working on a solution together, but in some cases, there are things you simply won't agree on or won't be able to convince them to support. Accepting instead of arguing is usually the right plan of action when you know you can't push the conversation any further.

SPEAKING TO YOUR SIBLINGS

Communicating with siblings is different from communicating with the adults in your house. Siblings are often relatively close in age and may even share a room. That level of closeness can sometimes make it easy to tell each other things. In fact, your siblings may even become your best friends as you grow up. However, being in the same space and knowing each other so well can cause its own set of problems. For example, siblings often tease one another.

In some cases, sharing embarrassing stories can be funny. If your sibling tells you that what you've said upset them, though, it's important to stop the teasing right away. Also, if you feel hurt by or uncomfortable with a comment or joke your sibling made—even if you know they didn't mean to hurt you—you can use the same clear and direct language that was proposed to stop teasing at school, such as "I don't think that's funny, and it makes me feel badly about myself. Please stop."

Siblings can often bring out some of our strongest emotions, so it's important to remember to manage those feelings when talking to them. Take a deep breath, calm yourself down, and work to understand their point of view while being clear about yours. Maybe your younger brother thought it was no big deal to "borrow" your expensive headphones without asking. Instead of yelling at him, look him in the eye, and calmly say, "I feel like I can't trust you when you take my things without asking. You need to ask me first." If you're not in attack mode, he'll be much more likely to hear the message and change his way of doing things.

Speaking to your siblings from a place of empathy is important. If you're the older sibling, try to remember how you felt when you were your younger sibling's age. If you're the younger sibling, realize that your older sibling could be dealing with issues that you will face soon enough. If you work to keep the lines of communication open, your older siblings will have a lot to teach you, and your younger siblings will come to you for advice.

SPEAKING WITH CONFIDENCE

It's normal for siblings to argue sometimes, but if you handle your differences and disagreements in a direct and empathetic way, you can build a stronger relationship.

SAYING "I'M SORRY"

Sometimes families fight. Arguments and misunderstandings happen, and feelings can get hurt. When this happens, it's important to know how to apologize. Along with "I'm listening," "I'm sorry" are two of the most powerful words in the English language. The truth is, everyone is going to need to know how to say them at some point in their lives, and while it's not always easy to say you're sorry, it's always important.

If you need to apologize to someone in your family, be honest about what you did wrong, but don't go on about what an awful person you are. That makes the person who was hurt feel responsible for making you feel better, which is the opposite of how the conversation should go. Don't make excuses or bring up the times someone else messed up. No matter how embarrassed or uncomfortable you feel, look the other person in the eye, and own up to the mistake.

Your body language and tone of voice are very important when

SPEAKING WITH CONFIDENCE

These communication strategies are helpful for dealing with other family members too, such as grandparents, cousins, or half-siblings. However, it's important to remember that every family is different and what works for one family—or even one member of your family—might not work for another family or another individual.

apologizing. Slouching, avoiding eye contact, and crossing your arms over your body make you seem reluctant to say you're sorry instead of sincerely apologetic. In addition, speaking in an angry tone or a tone that's very quiet might make the recipient of your apology feel that you don't actually want to be saying the words. Instead, speak in an even voice at your usual speaking volume, and stand or sit in an open posture.

When you apologize, be sure to choose your words carefully. Saying "I'm sorry you feel that way" implies that you don't think you did anything wrong. It's better to say, "I'm sorry for what I did. What can I do to make things right?" Taking responsibility for your words and actions—and clearly stating your intent to do better—is a mature way to handle problems in any relationship.

Setting Boundaries

Our family members sometimes feel as if they can treat us differently because they know us so well. However, just because your siblings have always teased you about your hair or your parents have always made you hug all your extended family members even though hugging people makes you uncomfortable, that doesn't mean it always has to be that way.

It's healthy to set boundaries with our family members. Boundaries are the limits we place on others in terms of how they treat us. They're the ways we define what is and is not acceptable behavior toward us.

Some boundaries are emotional, such as what people can tease you about. Other boundaries are physical, including who can touch you and what kind of physical contact is acceptable. For example, setting a boundary with your siblings might sound like this: "I know we share a bedroom, but when I have a friend over, we sometimes need to use that room to talk in private. Can you please knock before coming in when you know I'm in there with a friend?"

It can feel uncomfortable to talk about our boundaries, but it's an important part of confidently communicating our needs with the people around us. In addition, it's important to respect other people's boundaries. For example, if your sister asks you not to tease her about her braces, then you should respect her wishes.

FRIENDSHIP AND DATING

When you think about the people you most enjoy talking to every day, you probably think of your friends or the person you're dating (or want to date). Having meaningful conversations is an important part of developing close relationships with your peers—whether that's romantically or as friends. However, it can sometimes be difficult to know where to begin when sharing things about yourself with friends or while on a date. Honest, open communication is how we form new relationships and strengthen existing ones, but it's not always easy.

SPEAKING WITH CONFIDENCE

Learning how to clearly communicate what you feel and what you need in your relationships, including both friendships and romantic relationships, is an important part of building confidence as you grow up.

Sometimes it can feel easier to just send someone a message on social media or a text instead of talking to them face to face, especially when you want to address a problem with a friend or a crush that you hope might turn into a relationship. Easier doesn't always mean better, though.

FRIENDSHIP AND DATING

It's good to know how to communicate confidently in person to handle conflicts, build solid relationships, and feel more comfortable showing the people around you who you truly are.

BUILDING STRONG FRIENDSHIPS

It might seem scary to be put in a situation where you have to make new friends, such as starting at a new school or joining a new travel team for soccer. However, you might find your new best friend by putting yourself out there and introducing yourself. Stand up tall, make eye contact, and try to smile—even if you feel nervous. Take a deep breath to steady your voice, say hello, and tell people your name. That's all it takes to open the door to new friendships.

Even in friendships that have been a part of your life for a long time, communication is important. This is especially true when conflicts come up. For example, if your friend is dating someone new or has found a new friend group and seems to have forgotten about you, ask them if you can talk. When you talk to them, don't let your emotions get the best of you. Stay calm, and begin by saying you're happy they're happy. Then, you can say that you miss hanging out together like you used to. Don't attack your friend or the new person or people in their life. Hurtful comments will end any chance at productive communication. Once you've spoken, listen to what your friend says with an open mind. Remember that your goal is to fix the friendship, not

> The silent treatment might seem like a good way to let your friend know you're mad at them, but it's actually not a very helpful strategy for fixing what's broken in your relationship. Honest communication is the only way to rebuild friendships with an even stronger foundation.

to win an argument. In many cases, friends don't exclude or ignore each other on purpose, and by calmly and clearly stating that you feel left out, you will open the lines of communication so you can both make time for each other.

Friendships are some of the most important relationships you'll have in your life, so it's good to develop healthy communication skills with your friends. Even if you feel deeply hurt by something your friend did, try to remain focused on I-messages, such as "I feel hurt when you cancel our plans to spend time with your new volleyball teammates," instead of name-calling. Gossiping about friends you're having a conflict with is also not a very confident way to deal with disagreements. Bringing other people into the drama between the two of you generally only causes more problems. Instead, deal with the conflict directly, try to understand your friend's point of view, and address issues when they come up instead of letting them grow into bigger problems over time. This is the mature way to talk through challenges between friends.

THE DATING GAME

It's nerve-racking to ask somebody out on a date. Even if you've known this person for a while and you know they like you back, taking that next step can be scary. Practice projecting confidence through your body language before you talk to them. Also, practice taking deep breaths to help you stay grounded and to control how fast you're talking.

When you ask someone on a date, be clear about the activity and time and direct in your delivery. This projects confidence. For example, ask, "Would you like to see a movie with me this weekend?" Should the answer be "no," thank them for hearing you out, and leave it at that. Trying to convince someone to go out with you is a drain on both your energy and self-esteem, and it often makes the other person feel uncomfortable too.

Once you start dating, make sure you keep talking. That doesn't mean you have to tell the other person every thought that crosses your mind, but it does mean telling them about yourself, sharing stories about your day, and listening when they do the same. This is how you get to know each other better.

It's also important to talk about any problems that crop up, rather than letting bad feelings take root. Be clear about your expectations too. If one of you wants to date casually and the other wants more of a commitment, you need to find a compromise that works for both of you. You have to be honest—with yourself and with the person you're dating—if you want a relationship that can go the distance.

Whatever the situation, being honest should trigger the same response in the person you're dating. If they refuse

FRIENDSHIP AND DATING

It's important to set boundaries in romantic relationships just like you do with family members and friends, and it's important to respect the boundaries of someone you're dating. When boundaries aren't communicated clearly, problems arise.

to talk about something, don't force a conversation at that moment, but ask if you can talk about the issue later. A pattern of clamming up is a bad sign. No relationship can survive for long without a free flow of communication.

Finding a Balance

Sometimes it might seem as if the most important thing in the world is finding someone to date, and romantic relationships are often an important part of growing up. However, friendships shouldn't be forgotten in the face of finding people to date, and open communication in both romantic relationships and friendships can help everyone in your life feel like they matter.

For example, if your friend tells you that they're feeling left out now that you're dating someone, listen to them. If you value their friendship, communicate that to them clearly, and make a specific plan right then to hang out with just the two of you. In addition, if the person you're dating says they'd like to be able to spend more time with their friends, don't immediately get defensive. It's natural to want to spend a lot of time with someone you have strong feelings for, but it's healthy to have interests, relationships, and plans outside of each other too. With that in mind, you can come up with a kind of schedule to try to balance time with your friend groups and time with each other.

If the person you're dating tries to keep you from seeing your friends at all or makes you feel like you shouldn't spend time with anyone other than them, they're showing signs of controlling and possibly abusive behavior, and you should talk to a trusted adult about this as soon as possible.

In some cases, the problems in a relationship are too big to overcome, or outside challenges such as distance get in the way. If you have to end a relationship with someone who has been good to you, remember to repay that goodness even at the end. Respect and empathy are important. However, if you've thought long and hard about this and still believe it's time to move on, valuing your own needs is vital too. Find a quiet place to talk, and be certain about what you want to say before you meet. That makes it easier to stand your ground if they try to change your mind. Be direct but kind, and remember that it's best to be honest about what didn't work without being cruel.

STANDING UP TO PEER PRESSURE

Everyone has a need to belong and to feel accepted, especially in friend groups and around someone they want to date. The pressure to go along with the crowd can be strong, and the voices of what others want from and expect of us can be very loud. However, instead of simply listening to other people, you need to also learn to listen to your inner voice. Whether you call that your conscience or your gut, it's what tells you if your words and actions line up with your beliefs. When you're certain of what you believe, it's much easier to communicate those feelings to others.

Suppose your friends think it's OK to skip school occasionally. Maybe they make fun of how people look or talk. If you think this is wrong, say so. Statements such as "I

SPEAKING WITH CONFIDENCE

Standing up to peer pressure can sometimes feel lonely. However, it's good to remember that speaking your truth and voicing your values will ultimately lead to even better relationships in the long run with people who like you for who you really are.

FRIENDSHIP AND DATING

think it's important to be in school every day I can" or "I don't think we should pick on Alyssa because of her hair" will let your friends know what you believe and that you don't approve of their behavior.

Peer pressure can be especially strong in social situations such as parties. If people are drinking or smoking and expect you to do the same, a simple "No thanks" or "I'll pass" often gets people to stop pressuring you. If it still doesn't stop and it's making you feel uncomfortable, it's sometimes best to remove yourself from the situation by calling a parent or older sibling to pick you up. In addition, if someone you're dating ever tries to pressure you into doing something you're not comfortable doing, a direct and clear "No" is the best course of action. Your safety and comfort is more important than their bruised ego.

It's not easy to speak out like this. Others may make fun of you or refuse to talk to you altogether. You may find that you're no longer invited to certain parties. The person you're dating might even break up with you or try to make you feel guilty for communicating your boundaries. It's OK to work to repair those relationships if you believe they can be improved. However, in the long run, staying true to who you are and speaking honestly about what you know you need, believe, and deserve are the most important things. When you communicate your values clearly, you might push some people away, but they're often not people who should be a big part of your life. Instead, over time, your openness about your values will draw good people to you, and your friendships and romantic relationships will be healthier and stronger because of it.

THE WORDS TO USE AT WORK

Communication in the workplace requires its own set of important skills. The ways you speak to coworkers, bosses, and customers are often very different from the ways you speak to family, friends, and classmates. It might seem as if learning how to speak confidently at work is a skill to put into practice later in life—used only by adults giving presentations in fancy office buildings. However, the basics of strong workplace communication are necessary to know even for part-time jobs after school and internships for class credit.

Like all forms of verbal communication, speaking to people at work is most

SPEAKING WITH CONFIDENCE

A job often puts you in contact with many different kinds of people, and it's good to learn how to confidently communicate with all of them.

effective when it's done with a clear goal in mind. On the job, that goal is often very clear—whether it's getting hired in the first place, asking your boss for a raise or time off, or helping a customer. Finding the right words and the right way to deliver them at work requires practice, but it's an important part of securing a job and building the foundation for a successful career.

ACING THE INTERVIEW

Job interviews are common sources of anxiety, but preparation and practice are the keys to overcoming the nerves and appearing confident. Prepare for the interview by researching the company and coming up with some set answers to common questions. You don't want to look like you're following a script, but you don't want to be surprised by basic questions either. When you put in the effort to research the company you're interviewing with, you come across as knowledgeable and enthusiastic. The way you present yourself speaks volumes to a potential employer. With that in mind, take care to dress professionally too.

Watch your body language as soon as you enter the workplace. When the interviewer greets you, look them in the eye, shake hands, and stand up straight to project confidence. Once you're seated, don't slump in your chair or stare off to the side. The way you carry yourself throughout the meeting will make a big impression on the interviewer. Make sure it's a positive one.

SPEAKING WITH CONFIDENCE

Projecting confidence is an important part of a job interview, but talking about your strengths isn't always easy or comfortable. Practice listing your achievements and making the case for why you'd be the best candidate for a job so that you feel good about yourself heading into the interview.

During the interview, listen actively to what the interviewer is saying. Give concise answers to any questions you're asked. Your goal is to show how your talents will help the company where you're hoping to work. It's a good idea to ask questions too, as this underscores your interest in the position. Show curiosity about a new product they're releasing, or mention some other information you've gathered from your research. Don't begin the interview by asking about benefits or employee discounts. Although those questions are legitimate, if you lead with them, you'll come across as focused on your needs rather than the needs of the company.

After the interview is done, thank the interviewer for the opportunity. Also, don't forget to send a follow-up letter or email to thank them again and reiterate why your background makes you the right candidate for the job. Check for typos, and maintain a professional tone. Keep that same sense of professionalism if you're called back for another round of interviews. Even if you feel more comfortable, continuing to treat everyone involved in the interview process with the utmost respect can help you seem confident but not cocky.

COMMUNICATION ON THE JOB

Once you get the job, work hard to create a great first impression. Be polite to everyone you meet and attentive when your boss and coworkers speak to you. If you have questions, make sure to ask them instead of holding back out of fear of seeming incompetent, and repeat back what you've heard to verify the answers to your questions.

Your strong communication skills should earn you a great reputation at work. That doesn't mean there won't be conflicts, though, but what matters is how you handle them. For example, if a coworker takes a break every 10 minutes and expects you to always cover for them, ask to speak to that person away from other employees. No matter how upset you're feeling, don't yell, "You don't do your job, so I get stuck doing it for you!" Instead, try a comment like "I feel stressed when I have to take on extra work. How can we support each other so that we both feel like we're doing our fair share?" This could lead to a solution, or it could be that your coworker is unwilling to acknowledge that they've added to your workload. In a case where these denials continue, you may need to get your supervisor involved.

In addition to coworkers, customers are important people to learn to communicate with. Whether you work at a store,

THE WORDS TO USE AT WORK

Working in the service industry, such as at a restaurant, often means interacting with people who expect you to be helpful and pleasant no matter what else happened to you that day. It's not always easy to put aside your problems. However, being able to manage your emotions to communicate without being rude or short-tempered is an important part of being mature and responsible—on the job and in others areas of life too.

restaurant, or hotel, the way you treat customers affects the success of a business. When you work in this type of environment, being friendly and upbeat is key. Let customers know that you are willing to help with any concern, large or small. Set that positive tone early, check in occasionally, and always focus on their needs. However, should a customer become aggressive toward you, seek the help of a supervisor. Pay attention to how your boss handles the situation so that you can learn how to defuse future heated conflicts.

LIKE A BOSS

Your boss is an authority figure and should be treated as such. That doesn't mean they can't be approached if you have a question or concern. When you do approach them, though, be direct and concise in your language. Your boss most likely has to answer many questions and handle many concerns every day, so keeping your request for time off or your question about the new computer system brief and focused shows you respect their time. This will often get you a more favorable response than whining, making demands, or taking too much time to make your point.

As in all communication, be honest and direct with your supervisor. For example, when asking for a raise, be clear about your accomplishments and the reasons why you deserve a pay increase. You may even want to bring a list of bullet points to read from should you get nervous. If your boss says no to your request, don't respond from a place of anger. Thank them for their time, and collect your thoughts on your own before deciding if you should start looking for a new job with better pay. Showing your frustration in front of your boss won't make them any more likely to give you a raise now or in the future.

Pay close attention to how your boss communicates to you and to the other people they interact with every day. If

Social Anxiety

It can sometimes be hard to communicate with confidence at work or school. Being nervous about a job interview, a presentation, or making new friends is normal and often expected. However, for some people, this anxiety is so severe that it interferes with their daily life.

People who have an intense fear or anxiety surrounding social situations—to the point of avoiding them altogether or experiencing debilitating physical symptoms of anxiety such as trouble breathing or nausea—have social anxiety disorder, which is sometimes known as social phobia. People with this disorder often worry about embarrassing themselves in front of others or being judged by others. They're not shy or awkward, although these are labels they're sometimes unfairly given by others. Social anxiety disorder is a serious mental health concern and should be taken seriously.

Treatment for this disorder often includes therapy and can sometimes include medication too. If you're dealing with this disorder, speaking to anyone—let alone speaking with confidence—might feel impossible. However, with the right treatment, speaking up in social situations without fear will feel easier.

SPEAKING WITH CONFIDENCE

Speaking with confidence is a skill that takes patience and practice to master. Your boss, your teachers, and other adults around you are often great sources of additional advice on becoming a more confident speaker.

they're a good boss, you'll be able to learn a lot from them. A big part of developing confidence in your communication skills is knowing that there's always more to learn—and that you can often learn those things by paying attention to the people around you. If your best friend has a good relationship with your strict science teacher, pay attention to how she answers questions and asks for extra help. If your older sister has been dating the same person for years, ask her for advice on how they communicate. If your boss is very successful, listen to how they talk to customers and handle conflicts between employees. Everyone can learn to speak with confidence, and it starts by being open to improving your communication skills in small ways every day.

MYTHS and facts

MYTH
If you avoid talking about a problem, it will eventually go away.

FACT
If a problem is troubling enough to cause conflict in a relationship, it can only be resolved through open and honest discussion. Although you might need a cooling-off period after a heated exchange, at some point you have to talk with the other person to try to come up with a solution that meets both of your needs.

MYTH
Communication skills can't be learned. Some people just naturally like talking more than others.

FACT
There is a world of difference between "talking" and truly communicating. Effective communication involves a wide range of skills that can only be developed through practice and a commitment to expressing oneself with both clarity and compassion.

MYTH
Good communicators always put the needs of others above their own.

FACT
One of the most important parts of effective communication is empathy. Empathetic people are more attuned to the needs of others and are more likely to try to meet those needs. However, that doesn't mean good communicators neglect their own needs. Effective communication is about respect, and that includes self-respect. If someone isn't treating you kindly or isn't respecting your boundaries, the most effective way to communicate with them is to tell them to stop and clearly state your needs in that situation.

GLOSSARY

advocate To speak in support of something or argue for something.

anxiety Fear or nervousness about something that might happen.

assumption Something that is believed to be true or probably true but that is not known to be true.

benefit Something extra (such as vacation time) that is given by an employer to workers in addition to their regular pay.

CEO The person who has the most authority in an organization or business.

concise Using few words and not including extra or unnecessary information.

confidentiality Privacy.

contradict To be or say the opposite of something that has been done or said.

curriculum The courses taught at a school.

debilitating Causing an inability to function.

defuse To make something less serious, difficult, or tense.

ego A person's opinion of themselves.

elective A class that is offered but not required for a course of study at a school.

gesture A movement of the body that shows or emphasizes an idea or a feeling. Also, to make such a movement.

incompetent Not able to do a good job.

initiative A first step toward a goal. Also, the energy shown in taking that step.

internship An educational or training program that gives experience for a career.

legitimate Fair or reasonable.

LGBTQ+ Referring to a group made up of people who identify as a gender different from the sex they were assigned at birth or who want to be in romantic relationships that aren't only male-female. "LGBTQ" stands for lesbian, gay, bisexual, transgender, and queer or questioning.

moderator Someone who leads a meeting.

nausea The feeling you have in your stomach when you think you are going to vomit.

patronizing Showing you believe you are more intelligent or better than other people.

reiterate To repeat something you have already said.

retaliation The act of getting back at someone who has hurt you or treated you badly by hurting them.

tailor To make or change something so that it meets a special need or purpose.

therapy The treatment of mental illness through talking with a professional about your problems.

underscore To show the importance of something.

verify To show or find out that something is correct.

vital Extremely important.

FOR MORE INFORMATION

American Psychological Association
750 First Street NE
Washington, DC 20002
(800) 374-2721
Website: www.apa.org
The American Psychological Association provides resources
	to deal with stress, social anxiety, bullying, and
	communication issues at school, work, and home.

Center for Nonviolent Communication
1401 Lavaca Street, #873
Austin, TX 78701
(505) 244-4041
Website: www.cnvc.org
The Center for Nonviolent Communication is a global
	organization that supports the learning and sharing
	of nonviolent communication skills and helps people
	peacefully and effectively resolve conflicts in personal,
	organizational, and political settings.

Girls Inc.
120 Wall Street, 18th Floor
New York, NY 10005
(212) 509-2000
Website: girlsinc.org
Girls Inc. is devoted to the development of the next generation
	of female leaders, and its mission includes fostering the
	development of confidence in young women.

National Communication Association
1765 N Street NW
Washington, DC 20036
(202) 464-4622
Website: www.natcom.org
The National Communication Association studies all forms, modes, and consequences of communication.

StopBullying.gov
U.S. Department of Health and Human Services
200 Independence Avenue SW
Washington, DC 20201
Website: www.stopbullying.gov
This initiative by the U.S. government provides both young people and adults with resources to help stop bullying—both if they're being bullied themselves and if they witness or learn about someone else being bullied.

The Trevor Project
PO Box 69232
West Hollywood, CA 90069
TrevorLifeline: 1-866-488-7386
Website: www.thetrevorproject.org
The Trevor Project is an organization dedicated to helping young members of the LGBTQ+ community feel safe and supported. Its TrevorLifeline, TrevorChat, and other resources connect young members of the LGBTQ+ community with people who will listen to them without judgment as they communicate their concerns, beliefs, and questions.

FOR FURTHER READING

Anderson, Chris, and Lorin Oberweger. *Thank You for Coming to My TED Talk: A Teen Guide to Great Public Speaking*. New York, NY: Houghton Mifflin Harcourt, 2020.

Bjorklund, Ruth. *The Science of Quiet People: The Shy Guide to the Biology of Being Bashful*. North Mankato, MN: Compass Point Books, 2019.

Burling, Alexis. *Healthy Romantic Relationships*. Minneapolis, MN: ABDO Publishing, 2021.

Currie-McGhee, L. K. *Getting a Job*. San Diego, CA: ReferencePoint Press, Inc., 2020.

Ellsberg, Michael. *The Power of Eye Contact*. New York, NY: HarperPaperbacks, 2010.

Fitzsimons, Kate. *The Teen's Guide to Social Skills: Practical Advice for Building Empathy, Self-Esteem, & Confidence*. Emeryville, CA: Rockridge Press, 2021.

Folger, Joseph P., Marshall Scott Poole, and Randall K. Stutman. *Working Through Conflict: Strategies for Relationships, Groups, and Organizations*. New York, NY: Routledge, 2021.

German, Kathleen M. *Principles of Public Speaking*. New York, NY: Routledge, 2020.

Johnson, Robin. *Above and Beyond with Communication*. New York, NY: Crabtree Publishing Company, 2017.

Jones, Joy. *Fearless Public Speaking: A Guide for Beginners*. New York, NY: SparkNotes, 2019.

Kay, Katty, Claire Shipman, and JillEllyn Riley. *The Confidence Code for Girls: Taking Risks, Messing Up, & Becoming Your Amazingly Imperfect, Totally Powerful Self*. New York, NY: Harper, 2018.

Knowles, Sue, Bridie Gallagher, and Hannah Bromley. *My Intense Emotions Handbook: Manage Your Emotions and Connect Better with Others*. London, UK: Jessica Kingsley Publishers, 2021.

Kuromiya, Jun. *The Future of Communication*. Minneapolis, MN: Lerner Publications, 2021.

Lynch, Amy. *Understanding Families: Feelings, Fighting & Figuring It Out*. Middleton, WI: American Girl Publishing, 2019.

Rand, Casey. *Communication*. Chicago, IL: Raintree, 2012.

Randy, Charles. *Communication Skills*. Broomall, PA: Mason Crest, 2019.

Reeves, Diane Lindsey, Connie Hansen, and Ruth Bennett. *Communication*. Ann Arbor, MI: Cherry Lake Publishing, 2021.

Santoro, Marisa. *Own Your Authority: Follow Your Instincts, Radiate Confidence and Communicate as a Leader People Trust*. New York, NY: McGraw Hill Education, 2021.

Skeen, Michelle. *Communication Skills for Teens: How to Listen, Express & Connect for Success*. Oakland, CA: Instant Help Books, 2016.

Spilsbury, Louise. *Family Issues? Skills to Communicate*. New York, NY: Enslow Publishing, 2019.

INDEX

A

abuse, as cause for communication problems, 37
active listening, 9, 21, 63
aggressiveness, 5, 17, 66
anger, 15, 17, 19, 40
anxiety, 4, 9, 17, 19, 20, 28, 34, 61, 67
apologizing, 5, 43–45
arguments, 43, 51
authority figures, respecting, 22, 66

B

balancing friendships and romantic relationships, 54
belittling others, 13, 27
body language, 12, 43, 52, 61
boss/supervisor, speaking with, 5, 6, 59, 61, 64, 66–68
boundaries, setting, 4, 46, 53, 58
bullying, 7, 9, 15–19, 29, 33
bullying policies at school, 17

C

calm, staying, 4, 15, 19, 20, 26, 38, 40, 41, 49, 51
club moderators, 31
coaches, speaking with, 21, 22, 23, 26, 31, 32, 33
comforting others, 5
communication, definition of, 4
controlling/abusive behavior, 54
coworkers, speaking with, 6, 59, 64
crossing your arms, 26, 45
customers, speaking with, 59, 61, 64–66
cyberbullying, explanation of, 16

D

dating/asking someone out, 4, 6, 47–49, 51–55, 57–58
defensiveness, 25, 40, 54
depression, 34
divorce, as cause for communication problems, 37
drinking alcohol, 57

E

embarrassment, 14, 16, 18, 19, 24, 41, 43, 67
emotional boundaries, explanation of, 46
emotions, strong, dealing with, 19–20, 41
empathy, 8, 9, 14, 40, 41, 42, 55, 69
ending a relationship, 55
eye contact, 10, 18, 40, 43, 45, 49, 61

F

facial expressions, 12
family counseling/therapy, 37
family dinners, 36

family meetings, 39
fear/being afraid, 10, 24, 27, 28, 31, 33, 49, 52, 64, 67
feelings, hurt, 4, 16, 17, 41, 51
friends, making, 6, 7, 15, 49, 59, 67
friends, speaking with, 4, 5, 47–51, 54
frustration, 19, 20, 27, 66

G

game nights, 36
gender identity nonacceptance, as cause for communication problems, 37
gestures, 10, 12
goals of a conversation, 22, 38, 50, 61, 63
gossiping, 51
group projects, 7, 9, 10–15, 19
guidance counselors, questions to ask, 30
guidance counselors, speaking with, 21, 27–31, 32, 34

H

hair, playing with, 12
help, asking for, 4, 5, 24, 27, 31–34
honesty, 26, 29, 31, 43, 47, 50, 52, 55, 58, 66, 69

I

I-messages/I-statements, 17, 26, 27, 51, 55–57
inner voice/conscience, listening to, 55
interrupting, 25

J

job interviews, 61–64, 67
judging others, 9, 67

K

kindness, 16–17, 55, 69

L

learning from others, 68

M

maturity, 34, 45, 51, 65
mental health, 28, 33, 34, 67
mentors, 34
misunderstandings, 4, 43

N

negative emotions, 19–20
nervousness, 12, 49, 66, 67
nonverbal communication, 12

O

Obama, Barack, 6
openness, 9, 31, 40, 41, 47, 50, 54, 58, 68, 69

P

parents, speaking with, 4, 5, 35–40
patronizing others, 5
peer intervention, 18–19
peer pressure, 55–58
physical boundaries, explanation of, 46
physical bullying, explanation of, 16
practicing, 5, 6, 10, 11, 21, 52, 61, 62, 68, 69
preparing/being prepared, 10, 61
presentations, 4, 9–10, 67
psychologists, 28, 32, 34
public speaking classes, 9

R

respect, 8, 22, 23, 25, 26, 55, 64, 69

S

sadness, 17, 29
safety, 9, 18, 31, 33, 58
scowling, 26
self-respect, 8, 69
service industry, working in, 65
siblings, speaking with, 5, 35–37, 40–41, 42, 46
silent treatment, 50
slouching, 45, 61
smoking, 57
social anxiety disorder, 67
social bullying, explanation of, 16
social media, 48
social phobia, 67
speaking to others
 boss/supervisor, 5, 6, 59, 61, 64, 66–68
 coaches, 21, 22, 23, 26, 31, 32, 33
 coworkers, 6, 59, 64
 customers, 59, 61, 64–66
 friends, 4, 5, 47–51, 54
 guidance counselors, 21, 27–31, 32, 34
 parents, 4, 5, 35–40
 siblings, 5, 35–37, 40–41, 42, 46
 teachers, 4, 5, 21, 22–27, 31, 32, 33, 37
speeches, 4, 6, 9–10, 12
standing/sitting up straight, 10, 45, 49, 61

T

teachers, speaking with, 4, 5, 21, 22–27, 31, 32, 33, 37
teasing, 15–18, 19, 40–41, 46
texting, 16, 48
thank-you letters/emails, 63
thinking before speaking, 4
trust, 12, 18, 19, 22, 29, 31, 33, 37, 41, 54

U

uncomfortable, feeling, 16, 32, 41, 43, 46, 52, 57

V

values, 56, 58

verbal bullying, explanation of, 16
voice, tone and volume of, 10, 12, 18, 19, 26, 38, 43, 45

W

whining, 26, 66

PHOTO CREDITS

Cover jeffbergen/iStockphoto.com; p. 6 David Peterlin/Shutterstock.com; pp. 8, 11, 24–25, 36–37, 38–39, 44–45, 68 Monkey Business Images/Shutterstock.com; pp. 14–15, 16, 60 SpeedKingz/Shutterstock.com; pp. 22–23 Rawpixel.com/Shutterstock.com; pp. 28–29 VH-studio/Shutterstock.com; pp. 32–33 Sabphoto/Shutterstock.com; pp. 42–43 Lopolo/Shutterstock.com; pp. 48–49 Syda Productions/Shutterstock.com; pp. 50–51 antoniodiaz/Shutterstock.com; p. 53 Antonio Guillem/Shutterstock.com; pp. 56–57 fizkes/Shutterstock.com; pp. 62–63 mentatdgt/Shutterstock.com; p. 65 Iakov Filimonov/Shutterstock.com.

Editor: Katie Kawa
Designer: Michael Flynn